Escape into Nature...
and Soothe your Soul

Diane M. Hibbard, BA, BSEE, LMT, RYT

A Meditative Soul Publication

Copyright ©2021 by Diane M. Hibbard
ISBN: 978-1-7369620-1-5
All photographs and writings are the works and property of Diane Hibbard.
All rights reserved.

No part of this book may be reproduced or transmitted in any form or by any means, without written permission from
Diane Hibbard and Meditative Soul.

Published by Meditative Soul
42 Meadow Glen
Fairport, NY 14450
www.meditativesoul.com

Please reach out to
contact@meditativesoul.com
for permission to use any part of this book.

*For my girls...
Christa, Michelle, and Holly
who are my heroes, my inspiration, my strength,
my loves, and my heart. I am grateful for every
moment I get to be your Mom.*

*For my Mom, Dad, and family, who've shown me how
to love, laugh, and endure life with optimism and faith.*

*And finally, this book is dedicated
to all those I love...*

You know who you are. You have seen me take
countless of pictures of you, smile at you,
hike with you, hold you in thought and prayer,
reach out to you, and love you from near and far.
Hopefully, you have felt
my presence with you in Spirit
on this journey we share together.

*I see you. I feel your heart.
I love you.*

Note to the reader:

This book contains years of my journey, years of my heart searching for beauty in all I see, seeking comfort in Nature and God... and has come to be, by my desire and hope, to comfort others.

I often feel I am in on a secret that God has shared with me: to see all the beauty in creation and to marvel at the many miracles it holds. I believe this beauty is open to all of us, when we can just stop, pause, breathe, and wait for it to unfold. I pray that these pages allow you moments to feel held in the secrets that God shares and instills in the beauty of each living thing. All that is here, comes from hours of observing, searching, and seeking God's comfort, and in marveling at God's beautiful creations. Please join me on each page, taking your time as I did, so we can walk along the path together.

With my love and my heart,
Diane

Tips on how to use this book:

This book is intended to give you an escape. It provides a chance to pause and move away from the stresses of everyday life, and to help you take a moment of self-care to meditate on God's beauty. When practiced over time, the beauty in this book will help to heal your heart and soothe your soul.

There is no one right way to go through this book, but I do encourage you to reserve a moment each day to pause on a picture or a thought and take your time with what might come up for you. Many people feel that it is too difficult to meditate, or clear their mind, but meditation can also be practiced by focusing on beauty, a thought, a mantra.

These pages are intended to move you towards meditation and it's many calming and centering effects; by giving you a chance to experience God's beauty as a way to take a break in your busy day. Nature has such wonderful healing powers, but often our lives don't allow us to escape to it as often as we would like. Keep this book close to you, and open it often. When you find the stress of your day ruling your thoughts and emotions, this will help you to calm your nervous system, and move you to a more centered place in your decisions, your actions, and your life.

Start with one or two pages at a time… and take your time… to see what may come up for you as you move through your healing journey.

Please feel free to reach out to me with any questions or feedback on my website: www.meditativesoul.com, Facebook (https://www.facebook.com/meditativesoul) or Instagram (@meditativesoul3).
I would love to hear from you.

It's a simple walk from here to there, one that takes a matter of minutes. But the changes that occur as you wind your way through the trees, are anything but simple. As if transformed by the wisdom found within their rings, you shed your thoughts and worries.

Your breathing starts to ease...
                Your pace slows...
                          Your spirits lift...

For in this space where nothing is expected, nothing is needed...
You simply place one foot in front of the other.

Then as if touched by Divine grace, your senses open to the beauty that surrounds you. Your heart takes it all in, joyfully anticipating the adventures that lie ahead.

It's a simple walk, from here to there.

If you could

escape into

nature...

where would

you go?

I will be a painting."

Come...

Stay...

Rest...

Good morning ...

It looks like all the trees got up early to see the sunrise.

What are weeds to some...

are flowers to others.

When on a quest to find your favorite leaf... you may discover you love them all.

Is it time?

Yes, it's your time to shine.
You are so beautiful.

What helps you get through the twists and turns in life?

```
              H
              O   L O V E
         F    P
       GRATITUDE
         I
         T
         H
```

Take a moment to appreciate your resilience even during times of struggle or loss. Recognize where you receive support, and where you gain strength.

        Take a moment to breathe...

            Take a moment for gratitude...

                Take a moment for you.

*Can you see it?
The beauty beyond the blowing leaves?*

Can you see it?
The beauty beyond the blowing leaves?

Sometimes it can be hard to see beauty when your thoughts are like blowing leaves, moving here and there, being constantly distracted, especially during difficult times. But maybe just for a moment, focus on the beauty and stillness away from the fray.

Try to find the peace that lies beyond and let it hold you, comfort you, and guide you on your journey forward.

When you notice your thoughts are running from here to there, take a moment to look outside, and focus on one thing...
a tree, a bird, the sky...
Can you see something that you find beautiful about it?
Do you notice the shift in your heart when you focus on the beauty?

That's it! That's the beauty beyond the fray.
You've found it!

"I'm grateful for you."

Everyone struggles in their own way, and needs faith and others for support. You are made to need others, so reach out to a trusted friend if you need to. It is beautiful to feel needed and loved.

"I'm grateful for you, too.
Thank you for being there and for being you."

Sometimes what you don't realize, is that others need you, too. Everyone is special in their own way and you have your own gifts to offer. It is often easier to see the value of others, but God made you, there is no one like you. You are beautiful and are the only one that can give the gift of you.

"I love you," said the sea
to the clouds in the sky.
"I wish I could drift along the shore..."

"Oh, but it is we who love you,"
said the clouds to the sea.
"Can you ebb and flow some more?"

"Oh, I love that you see the beauty in each other,
as I shine on you both with my light."
"But don't you see," said the Sun.
"That you're both dearly needed,
to make this scene just right!"

How far does your love flow?
From your heart...
To a loved one.
To a neighbor,
To a friend.
To your pet,
To wildlife.
To flowers,
To trees.
To birds,
To bees.

How far does your love flow?
From your heart...
To all people.
To this country,
To all lands.
To the depths of the ocean,
To the far reaches of space.
To this beautiful Earth,
To the glorious Heavens.

How far does your love flow?
From your heart within...
To all living things.
With love...

"Look up,
dear one
look up..."

"The sky was painted just for you!"

Imagine you are climbing a mountain where each good thought, hopeful intention, belief of healing, and wishful dream moves you further up the slope. With every ounce of energy you use to focus on a positive moment, you gain strength to climb higher and higher. It's not that you ignore there's pain or worry below; it's that for now, you choose to climb, because you deserve to see the view.

When
Heaven smiles
and
Earth smiles
right back...

"Have you seen the sky, really seen the sky,
Where my heart abides to watch over thee?
From the shores below to the clouds above,
I share my love for all to see.

Have you seen my heart, really seen my heart,
With you, in all you do and see?
Come, walk along the shores below
And share your heart with me.

Can you feel my love, really feel my love,
As you walk along the shore?
During times when you are weary,
I can carry you some more.

Can you share my love, really share my love,
With all below and up above?
Because everything worth 'knowing,'
Begins and ends with love."

With Love,
The Divine

What if snowflakes are blessings from Heaven, covering all in a blanket of love...

And maybe snow is slippery to encourage you to slow down and pause long enough to appreciate its beauty...

And what if each snowflake's ability
to float quietly to the ground
is to help bring you peace?

"I'm going to rest here, you see
On a branch in a tree,
And watch the snow float down
and sit next to me.

I'm going to rest here, you see
In the still of the tree,
And find a moment of peace,
A place to just be...

I'm going to rest here, you see
In the beauty of the tree,
Come sit nearby,
And breathe with me...

I'm going to rest here, you see
With you and the tree,
And share in the joy,
Of all we see..."

"Snow, I welcome you to my branches,
Where you can sit and rest.
For it's with your glistening beauty,
That I can look my best."

"Tree, thank you for your kindness
As you break me from my fall.
For together we share beauty
And love and peace with all."

Put your hand over your heart and feel the peace flow in and through you...

Sometimes, if you look closely, you can catch the *clouds painting leaves*...

Imagine...

If you could rest on a hill,
Under a cross,
With a deer?

And pray for healing,
Pray for love,
Pray for goodness,
And grace from above.

For in this moment,
You could rest,
And allow for God
To do what's best.

For in Her hands
You would not miss,
Your glorious chance
To find true bliss.

Wherever this journey takes you,
remember you are not alone.

Frozen in time... the leaves are still hanging onto the tree even though the lake is frozen and the seasons have changed. Maybe they are waiting for you to notice their beauty, their resilience, their presence. Even though everything around them has changed... maybe they are still waiting for you, so you can move forward together...

Ahhh, in stillness, is peace...

Sometimes, life feels like a puzzle, where you need to figure out how all the pieces fit together... which pieces to use and which to set aside. And at times, some pieces don't seem all that pretty... some when put together, seem messy... and others even seem to be missing. But what if those "not too pretty" pieces, and the messiness, have an inner beauty and purpose that will be revealed over time? What if the missing pieces leave room for God to transform everything into something more beautiful than you could ever imagine...

Can you feel Angels watch over you and guide you?

When you need reassurance,
look to the Heavens...

Trees, what are you doing?"

"We're reaching for you!"

"That's so beautiful, but you know I'm always with you, around you, and within you… all you need to do is pause to feel my presence."

"Well, with all that's going on, how will we know it's you?"

"Ah, when you take a moment to notice the stillness that surrounds and holds you, when you feel a glimpse of peace, that's me…

I love when you reach for me, but I'm always there, always around you, always within you… just know, I've already reached for you."

Take a moment to feel the tenderness,
the beauty, and the delicate glow...
the flower's gift to you.

Each petal, each leaf is so beautifully crafted,
so carefully made, and when they grow together,
they are a work of art intended to bring you joy.

You were made to fly... simply spread your wings.

Notice how the ripples on the water reveal that the breeze is gently moving toward you... coming to soothe and comfort you...

Sometimes it makes more sense to get lost in a moment, than to miss it altogether...

Somewhere out there is a dream, looking for you...

"I'll stand right here by your side
and watch over you."

Within you is an abundance of beauty, hope, and promise... just waiting for the right moment...

When you look at this picture,
you might not notice the tree on top of the mountain.
It may seem small and insignificant.
But to the tree, its mere presence is a victory against all odds
and most likely, it feels on top of the world.
Perspective is everything...

Believe, the possibilities are endless...

Look within yourself...
to find your inner strength...
to tap into your inner wisdom...
to free your spirit.

The Contemplative Cormorant

"And here I'll sit...
What's before me... can wait
What's behind me... is free
For this is all I have...
all I am, and all I'll be.
So here, I'll sit...and take my time,
For just a moment on my quest...
For it's in the being-ness
and knowingness, I rest."

Let the rays of Hope...

... lead you out of darkness.

Come, rest in the beauty...

And breathe...

And then there's life, when you least expect it, throwing in those twists and turns. What does your road map look like... the planned and the unplanned? The destinations you planned to see, and did... those you thought you'd see, but didn't.... and those you never even imagined you'd see, that brought you to beautiful and unexpected places. It's all a part of your story... all a part of what makes you... you.

When life feels overwhelming and messy, a clear path forward can help provide a sense of purpose, comfort, and hope. What you sometimes need to remember is that the path forward is always there. It just isn't always clear or visible. But if you close your eyes and pause... take some time to rest in the silence, slow your breathing, and put your hand over your heart... comfort, faith, and hope emerge. Even if you don't see or know the path ahead. You know it's there... laid out in front of you. God knows the path forward. Trust He'll hold your heart and hand as He shows you the way.

Can you feel the warmth of Divine Love embracing you?

In moments when you have thoughts of "not doing enough," "not having enough," or "not being enough…" recognize that you were never intended to travel this journey alone. It was never about you doing everything, having everything, or being everything. These "holes" are openings… invitations for the Divine to help you, to fill you, and to join you on this path. So when you notice these thoughts and feelings crop up, open your heart. Invite God's love and light in to help you, to fill you, to comfort, soothe, and heal you… to "be" with you. You were never intended to take this path alone…

Wishing you comfort, love and peace,

Acknowledgments

I am so grateful for all the wonderful teachers, friends, and family who have supported me on this journey. A "thank you" seems so inadequate. I know it would be impossible for me to list every beautiful soul that has crossed my path, taught me so much, and been with me during my most trying times. I feel I have been so fortunate to have met such beautiful Angels here on Earth throughout my life, and for that I am forever grateful. You have each contributed in your own way to act as mentors and guides on your spiritual path, and I am thankful that you shared your journey with me.

For this specific book, I would love to thank my generous, wise, and talented editor and guide, Sheila Kennedy, for without her, this would have not been possible. Also, I'd like to thank Christine Baker-Marriage and Susan Carmen-Duffy, who each, in your own way had a vision of this for me, many years before I even thought it was possible. For that, and all the goodness each of you consistently brings to the world, I thank you.

For all my Therapists and Teachers: Massage Therapists, Myofacial Release Therapists, Psychotherapists, and Yoga Instructors, I thank you… for it was your passion and dedication that helped me peel back the layers to find the beauty within. This is just a small list of the many who touched my life.

John F. Barnes, PT, LMT, NCTMB
Maria de la Cruz, PT, LMT
Lori Zeltwanger, PT
Kori Tolbert, LMT, ISMETA
Dr. Vicky McCoy, DC
Cora Kannel Mayo, LMT

François Raoult, M.A., E-RYT500, C-IAYT
Judith Hanson Lasater, Ph. D., PT
Mary Aman, M.A., E-RYT 500
Julie Finer, LMT, NMT, RYT
Jane Fisher, LCSW

I'd like to include a special thank you to Kori Tolbert, who taught me what true vulnerability looks like. Through her work, life, and writings she has shown me, and all of us by example, how to face all of what life brings our way-and how to work through it, drop into it, and heal through it. Without her great work and writings, I wouldn't have had the courage to share my own vision and journey. Kori, your work, writings, and passion for healing, inspire me.

I'd also like to thank Bob, Christa, Michelle, and Holly for giving me the beautiful gifts of my camera and equipment. For without all of you, your generosity, and your patience, I wouldn't have been able to capture and fully see nature's beauty.

Finally, this book would not have been possible without Isha Das and all the beautiful souls at The Assisi Institute, who helped to lead me on the journey to finding my Guru, Paramahansaji Yogananda and Kriya Yoga. Your guidance and the work you do each and every day, has truly enhanced my connection to God, Jesus Christ, the Divine Mother, and all the Gurus in the lineage. Without Yogananda's teachings and guidance, I wouldn't have been able to truly see and appreciate the underlying beauty within all living things. I am so grateful to all of you, humbled by all you give to others, and grateful to all in the lineage who help guide us, watch over us, and move us all closer to the Divine.

And a heartfelt thank you to my family, friends, and my girls and their countless hours of patience... waiting and watching me take all these pictures and listening to my thoughts about all the beauty I see. You are all so patient and loving and for that I thank you. To all of you who have played such a special part in my journey, I thank you and give you my love...

Author Bio

Diane Hibbard is the Founder and Director of Meditative Soul, an organization specializing in bringing words and imagery together to help offer moments of meditation to provide comfort, support, and healing. Combining her unique skills as a Licensed Massage Therapist, Yoga Teacher, and Photographer with over 30 years of e-Learning design experience in developing training solutions, Diane brings all her skills and creativity to help share Nature's beauty with others. She practices Kriya Yoga, a spiritual meditative practice, and tries to bring Divine light and guidance into her work. Her wish is that her pictures and words can help you escape for just a moment, to help you heal, to bring you peace and hope, and to help you feel connected to the love that surrounds you each and every day.

For years, Diane has sought comfort in nature during times of stress, anxiety, and grief. She finds that each moment she has spent capturing Nature's beauty and pairing the image with words that came to mind during meditation, have helped with her healing process and has helped improve her overall health and well-being.

Diane's dream is that her work can help build an appreciation for seeing the beauty of the Divine in all, and that she can help give back to Nature and all living things.

Diane's work has been featured at Create Art 4 Good Gallery, and hangs in therapy offices, homes, and is used on social media by yoga studios to help provide comfort and peace to others.
Diane practices as a licensed massage therapist specializing in the John F. Barnes Myofascial Release techniques. She teaches gentle and restorative yoga, shares her photography and writings through Meditative Soul, and works as an e-Learning designer and developer under her business Media-Wright.

You can see more of her work at www.meditativesoul.com, Facebook (https://www.facebook.com/meditativesoul) Instagram (@meditativesoul3), or SmugMug (https://meditativesoul.smugmug.com).

www.ingramcontent.com/pod-product-compliance
Lightning Source LLC
Chambersburg PA
CBHW041703160426
43209CB00017B/1729